Marinara

Written by Kathy Jenkins
Illustrations by Jamie Cosley
Colors by Tyler Cosley
entire contents copyright 2015 Jamie Cosley

Avery has a magic garden.

And all the children know.

That when you plant a snowball.

A friendship starts to grow.

May I introduce you to Marinara?

A special friend of mine.

She is so sweet and very cute

And oh, so very kind.

A chubby cuddly pom-pom

That grew to be with me.

A walking, talking ball of snow.

For everyone to see.

She has a nose like a tomato.

Both red and very round.

14

She has a wig made of spaghetti.

That she loves to flip around!

Sledding in the winter.

Picking pumpkins in the fall.

In the springtime we'll hunt eggs.

I bet we find them all!

In the summer we'll go swimming.

We'll run and laugh and PLAY!

We'll spend our time together.

Every single day.

Made in the USA
Columbia, SC
23 November 2018